Caring for Your
PUPPY

by John and Mary Holmes

© 2012 Dalmatian Press, LLC
All rights reserved. Printed in China.

The DALMATIAN PRESS name is a trademark of
Dalmatian Press, LLC, Franklin, Tennessee 37067.
No part of this book may be reproduced or copied in any form
without the written permission of Dalmatian Press, LLC.
Editor *Mary Ginder*

CE19771/1111

About the Authors

Professional dog trainers John and Mary Holmes have spent a lifetime working with dogs—breeding them, caring for them, and training them. They have helped many handlers solve problems with their dogs, as well as training their own dogs for a wide range of tasks—from film and television work to obedience competitions and farm work. They have bred and shown pedigree dogs under their Formakin kennel name and they were responsible for importing the Australian Cattle Dog to Britain. John is an international championship show judge. He is a well-known contributor to the canine press and has written books on training the family dog and the working dog. Mary has served on the committee of the Australian Cattle Dog Society and has edited their newsletter for eight years.

Acknowledgement

Photographs have come from a number of sources and they have made a major contribution to the book. Thanks to Sally Anne Thompson for all the photographs on puppy care and training, to Steve Nash and Carol Ann Johnson for assorted pictures, and to the Metropolitan Police for the photo of a working German Shepherd Dog. Special thanks to the readers of *Dogs Today*, especially Linda Jury, who have allowed us to use photographs of their pet dogs, and to the magazine's editor, Beverley Cuddy, for her kind cooperation.

Contents

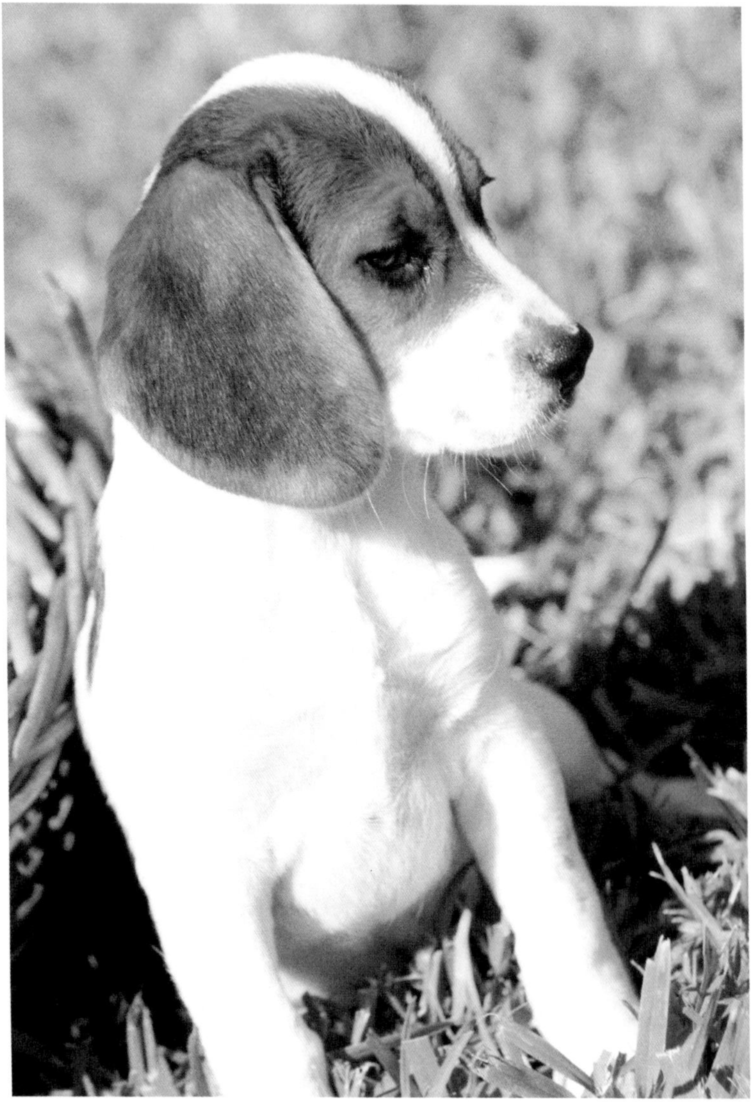

Petco
1701-59, 61 US RT 22 West
Watchung, NJ 07069
908-322-2844

2/22/13 7:02PM 1726 02 2 02/00
Sales Associate: 24   Tyler

ITEM	DESCRIPTION	PRICE
000825859	PUPPY WORKS	23.00 T
Ticket#:205419	GROOMER:083	CODE:40

Taxable Total $23.00
Tax 7.0000%   1.61

Sub Total $24.61
Final Total $24.61
Gift Card Redeemed   24.61
Acct# XXXXXXXXXXXX2419   Auth# 654478
Balance: $23.63

Number of Items   1

Pals Rewards Number: 425797046

T = Taxable   N = Non-Taxable
(1)Store Discount not subject to sales tax
(2)Manufacture coupon subject to sales tax

Thank you for shopping at Petco!
Questions/Comments?
888-824-7257

Petco provides information on
housing, equipment, cleaning,
environment and feeding for
all the animals we offer. Ask
for an in-store Care Sheet
or log onto www.petco.com.

1726024022700201302224257970465

initial purchase (please see store for details).

petco.

where the healthy pets go

Petco Return Policy

• Returned merchandise must be in its original condition and packaging. Merchandise not in its original condition and packaging that shows signs of use or abuse will not be accepted.

With a Valid Receipt:
• For returns made within 30 days of the initial purchase, we will give you a refund in the form of your original payment method.
• A Corporate Check will be issued for cash refunds over $300.
• For all returns made after 30 days of the initial purchase, we may issue you a Petco Gift Card.

Without a Valid Receipt:
• With valid identification, we will issue a Petco Gift Card for the sale price of the merchandise at the time of the return (please see an associate for details).

Aquatic Life Returns:
• There are no refunds for saltwater returns.
• Freshwater returns must be returned within 30 days of initial purchase.
• A water sample must accompany deceased aquatic life (please see an associate for details).

Companion Animal Returns:
• Companion animals may be returned within 15 days of initial purchase (please see store for details).

earn 5% back on everything you buy*

*Visit palsrewards.com for details.

petco.

where the healthy pets go

Petco Return Policy

• Returned merchandise must be in its original condition and packaging. Merchandise not in its original condition and packaging that shows signs of use or abuse will not be accepted.

With a Valid Receipt:
• For returns made within 30 days of the initial purchase, we will give you a refund in the form of your original payment method.
• A Corporate Check will be issued for cash refunds over $300.
• For all returns made after 30 days of the initial purchase, we may issue you a Petco Gift Card.

Without a Valid Receipt:
• With valid identification, we will issue a Petco Gift

1

STARTING OUT RIGHT

Bringing a puppy into your home is a major commitment. With luck, you are looking forward to a relationship that will last twelve to fourteen years, so your decision to buy or adopt a dog deserves to be well thought out. It's also important to select the puppy or dog which best suits your lifestyle. This animal will be dependent on you for the rest of its life and you must carefully consider whether you are prepared to accept the responsibilities which this involves.

Your Responsibilities

As an owner, your first responsibility is to the dog who, in return for the love and devotion he so willingly gives, deserves to enjoy a reasonable quality of life. A puppy needs mental as well as physical exercise. He needs to live like a dog, not like a human—rolling in the grass and, in permitted areas, being allowed to run freely without the restriction of a leash.

Your second responsibility is to other members of the community. You must ensure that the dog is under control at all times, and you must be prepared to clean up after your pet.

Small dogs like this Yorkshire Terrier are a good choice for those living in apartments, but they still need regular exercise and enjoy being outdoors.

All puppies look appealing, but consider their adult size. This young Rottweiler will grow into a large dog requiring plenty of exercise, a lot of food, and firm handling.

Your third responsibility is to yourself and to your family. Do all members of the family agree on getting a dog? Are you willing to devote the time and energy necessary to train the dog to make him a well-behaved member of the family?

The Right Start

Despite all the best intentions, the relationship between dog and owner can go wrong. In fact, most problems that dog owners have to cope with could, and should, be avoided by the use of a little common sense and by starting off with the right puppy. Perhaps the most important point to remember is that more can be learned about a puppy from his ancestry than from the puppy himself.

This is why there can be more security in buying a purebred puppy than a mongrel (or mutt). At least you have some idea of what the purebred puppy will grow up to look like, which is difficult to predict with a mongrel puppy.

However, people often make the mistake of assuming that all the puppies in a purebred litter will resemble the parents in temperament as well as looks, when the reality is far different.

The Importance of Inheritance

So which breed is right for you? There are some four hundred dog breeds worldwide, and books have been written about most of the better-known breeds. However, the weakness of some of these books is that they are written by enthusiasts who stress the good points of their favorite breed while down-playing the less favorable traits. It's important to take a more balanced view.

A puppy inherits her characteristics from both parents, but some of these traits are more inheritable than others.

It's important to see a puppy with its mother so you can get an idea of how your puppy will develop mentally and physically.

According to Dr. Malcolm Willis, a well-known geneticist, the most inheritable characteristic of all is fear. This is not surprising when we consider that the dog is descended from the wolf. The bold, fearless wolf would very soon be a dead wolf, while the shy, furtive wolf would live to pass its genes on to future generations. However, a fearful or nervous dog is almost invariably an unhappy dog. It can also be, and often is, a dangerous one. Nervous dogs are the most likely to bite, even if the person they bite is well known to them or a child.

For the first six weeks or so of her life, a puppy is entirely under the influence of her dam (mother). The pup will watch her mother and learn from the way she behaves. If the mother is outgoing and friendly, the pup will behave the same way. If the mother is nervous and fearful, the pup will copy these reactions. Experiments have shown that nervous mothers produce nervous puppies, even when the puppies are fostered by other females.

It's always best, if possible, to see a puppy with its mother. Initially, see how the mother reacts when you approach her puppies. If she is wary or aggressive, her young may be like that, too. Take time to look at lots of litters before you select a puppy. If you make the right choice, you will have many years of fun, pleasure, and companionship to look forward to. If you make the wrong choice, you will have years to regret it.

Preparations

Once you have decided to get a puppy, you will need to make quite a few preparations before bringing your new pet home. If possible, decide on the puppy's name in advance. Everything will be strange to him and if everyone in the family is trying out different names on him, he will only become confused. If you cannot come up with the right name initially, just call him "Puppy" until you do—chances are this is what he was used to being called by the breeder.

Check the safety of both house and yard to ensure there are no hazards for an inquisitive puppy. Trailing electrical wires are a magnet to pups and can cause fatal accidents. Flimsy coffee tables, standing lamps, and decorative items on low tables all constitute potential accidents waiting to happen. Store household cleaners, chemicals, insecticides, and medications safely. Keep anything harmful or valuable out of the puppy's reach.

Your yard should be well-fenced and puppy-proofed. Puppies are great escape artists, squeezing through the smallest of gaps with the greatest of ease. Be careful to keep pets away from insecticides, slug pellets, etc.

Buying Equipment

FEEDING BOWLS
Your puppy will need two bowls, one for food and one for water. Stainless steel bowls are recommended since they are virtually indestructible and easy to clean.

COLLAR AND LEASH (LEAD)
It is a good idea to get your puppy used to wearing a collar right from the start. Once he is used to a collar, you can start leash training. A light buckled leather or soft nylon collar is best, with a fairly long, light but strong leash.

BRUSH AND COMB

Few small puppies need much grooming. However, it is easier to train a young puppy to accept the grooming routine than it is to start a routine with an older dog. Groom your puppy even if she doesn't yet need it, particularly if she is a long-coated breed. At this stage, all you need is a good-quality brush and comb. Ask the puppy's breeder or your local pet supply store for recommendations on grooming equipment.

IDENTIFICATION

At the very least, your dog should wear a collar with identification tags bearing your current contact information. More permanent forms of identification include tattooing and microchipping. Many breeders now have their puppies tattooed before they are sold, and humane associations in some areas are offering community tattooing programs. This makes it easy to identify a stray dog so he can be returned to his owner. Your vet can also tattoo your dog. Another form of identification is a microchip, which is painlessly implanted under the loose skin between the dog's shoulders.

TOYS

A puppy must chew—it is part of growing up. There are a lot of canine chew toys available in pet stores. The best sort to buy are those made of hard rubber. Some nylon chew toys are also safe. Be sure that there are no pieces which can easily be dislodged or chewed off. Too many pups have to undergo surgery to remove indigestible pieces of rubber or small parts from chewing on unsuitable toys. If you are buying a ball, make sure it is large enough so that it cannot be swallowed.

You can buy knotted ropes in a variety of sizes, which most pups love to chew and pull on. Cardboard paper towel and toilet paper rolls are also popular toys for puppies.

Puppies need to chew—but that doesn't mean you want them to practice on your best shoes!

Offer safe, suitable toys which your puppy can chew while she is teething.

BEDS AND BEDDING

A warm draft-proof bed is essential. There are numerous types of dog beds on the market, but until the pup has stopped growing—and chewing—a plain cardboard box is perfectly adequate. Place the box on its side so that it makes a safe "den" for the puppy.

Bedding needs to be warm and washable. Synthetic fleece fabric is ideal since it reflects body heat, is non-allergenic and difficult to chew. It is also free-draining, which means that you can put newspaper under it and the upper side stays dry.

11

DOG CRATES

Last but not least, buy a folding dog crate. These can be expensive, but a good-quality crate will last a lifetime, and the benefit both you and your dog will get from it should far outweigh the initial expense.

By nature, dogs like to have a "den" which they can call their own. A crate makes a very satisfactory substitute. It is a great help with house training and makes a safe refuge for the puppy when she wants to sleep, eat her dinner, escape from tiny, clutching fingers, rowdy teenagers, or even from you, her owner, if you are busy or in a bad mood!

A dog who is used to a crate will learn to be relaxed when shut up in a confined space, so she will be much less stressed if she ever has to stay overnight at the vet or a boarding kennel.

Never use the crate for punishment. The whole idea is for the puppy to have a den of her own to enjoy. Do not shut her up for long periods during the day, but start with just a few minutes and gradually increase the time. If you are busy around the house or going out for a short while, put the puppy in the crate for safety, but remember that the crate is a place of temporary refuge—it is not your puppy's home.

A dog crate is an invaluable item of equipment. It gives the puppy a safe haven and is a useful aid for house training.

Finding a Vet

If you do not already know of a good veterinarian in your area, you will need to find one before your puppy arrives home. Ask your puppy's breeder or other dog-owning people in the neighborhood for recommendations.

Some puppies may have started a worming program and received their first inoculation, but you will need to find out what the local regulations are for vaccinations and what the vet recommends in regard to worming.

Bringing Your New Puppy Home

Try to bring your puppy home early in the day so that he will have time to settle in before evening. Take a friend or a member of the family along with you to help.

Be understanding. It is a little disconcerting to take the pup away from his mother and siblings and then put him in a crate all by himself and drive off. You want this puppy to like you and trust you, so, if it's not illegal where you live to have a loose animal in the car, we suggest that you settle the puppy in your friend's lap, or if it is a big puppy, let him lie next to your companion on the seat.

Put a collar and leash on your puppy. In the excitement of arriving home, the pup could easily slip out of the car, which is the last thing you need. Take along plenty of newspaper and old towels to spread around the puppy. Then, if the pup vomits (and he probably will), any mess can be cleaned up easily. Do not reprimand the puppy for being sick; it is not his fault.

Make sure you have all the necessary paperwork, such as vaccination certifications, record of worming, pedigree and transfer of ownership form (if applicable), and a certificate of tattooing or microchipping if this has been done. You will also need a diet sheet, and most breeders will supply you with enough food for the first few days.

It helps to have a friend along when you pick up your puppy and drive him home.

Let your puppy explore the yard when he first arrives home.

Arriving Home

Take the pup out quietly and let her explore the yard. Do not ask all your neighbors and friends to come and admire her, and try to pick a time when the children are at school. Your puppy will have quite enough to get used to without being overwhelmed by lots of new people.

Once the puppy has relieved herself, she can be taken into the house, preferably confined to a single room until she settles in and is house-trained. Offer the puppy a meal, play with her, and when she is relaxed and tired, let her sleep.

You can offer a meal, but do not worry if your puppy does not appear to be hungry. He will soon make up for lost time when he feels more settled.

The First Night

If you are using a crate, make sure it is ready with a bed inside and the door open. Your puppy can have his first meal there and you can encourage him to go in and explore, possibly having a nap there during the day.

At night, play a game with him in the hope of making him tired. Then take your puppy outside to relieve himself just before you go to bed. Put the pup to bed with a toy. He is bound to miss his siblings and the familiar surroundings.

We have found that a well-wrapped hot-water bottle (not too hot) and an old alarm clock, which will help to break the silence, can both be useful. The puppy will almost certainly whine or yap, but, if you are lucky, he will soon settle down.

Some pups keep on whining for hours and hours. Do not go and smack your puppy. He is not doing it to annoy you; he is simply homesick. Do not make the mistake, however, of going to give him a cuddle. This will just make him cry louder to see if you will come back again. If you really cannot stand the noise, take the puppy, in his crate, into your bedroom. Once he is used to the crate during the daytime you can gradually get him used to staying in another room at night. Do not take the puppy onto or into your bed. As he gets bigger, this is likely to be a habit you'll want to break!

House Training

All young animals born in nests want to keep their living quarters clean. This is why it is easy to house train a pig, but almost impossible to house train a chimpanzee!

Approached sensibly, house training should be no big problem. Do not start nagging at the puppy the minute you get him home and do not make a drama out of it. Puppies who have been properly reared, with the opportunity to go outside to relieve themselves, or those used to going on paper, are usually easy to teach.

First, decide on the area of the yard you want your puppy to use. Then choose a word or phrase to use to encourage him to do what you want—"hurry up" or "get busy," for example. It does not matter what you say, so long as you always use the same words. Never put the puppy out alone. Always go with him and stay with him until he performs. Tell him to "hurry up" (or whatever phrase you're using) in an encouraging tone, and as soon as he relieves himself, repeat the phrase and give him lots of praise.

Do not be in too much of a hurry to rush back inside. Many puppies and adult dogs eliminate more than once, so give your puppy a chance to relieve himself completely. Then have a short game and go back inside. You should soon be able to judge how long you need to stay out with the puppy.

To start with, your puppy will be unable to last all through the night without relieving himself. Some conscientious owners get up during the night and take the puppy outside, which undoubtedly speeds up house training. But do not worry if you are not the sort who relishes waking up at 2:00 a.m. Leave some newspaper on a rubber mat or plastic sheet on the floor and, if your puppy dirties the paper during the night, just clean it up. He should eventually grow out of this.

To avoid mistakes during the day, shut the pup in his crate if you are too busy to keep an eye on him. As already stated, do not leave him for too long, and if you hear him scratching or whining, hurry back and take him out. If your puppy makes a mistake in the house when you are not there, do not punish him when you return as he will have no idea what he did wrong.

Occasionally, a puppy may not seem to have inherited the instinct to be clean, or the instinct has been weakened because the puppy has been forced to live under conditions where he had no alternative to toileting close to his sleeping and eating areas. With this pup you will need to be even more vigilant. As soon as you see any signs of him squatting, pick him up very quickly, telling him "no" in a harsh voice, and take him outside. Do not shout—it will not help. Stay with the puppy, even if it is a long wait. Tell him to "hurry up," and when he finally performs, make a big fuss over him, telling him how clever he is.

LEARNING TO READ THE SIGNS

Your pup will need to go out after every meal, after a drink, as soon as he wakes up, after a game, and any other times he shows signs of uneasiness. Puppies usually give signs of wanting to relieve themselves. Some turn around and around, others sniff the ground, scratch, look around, whine, or suddenly squat down. An observant owner—and you will need to be one—soon learns the signals.

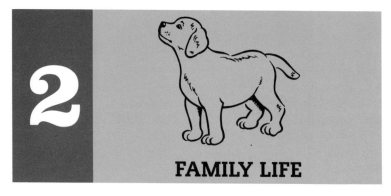

FAMILY LIFE

Puppies and Children

Puppies and children growing up together can form lasting and rewarding relationships. It has been proven that children who play with animals early in life tend to be more open-minded and make more effort to understand others than children who have not had this opportunity.

However, you must use common sense. No matter how accustomed to dogs your children are, nor how good-tempered your puppy, never leave a small child or baby alone with a puppy. Disasters can —and do—happen very quickly. A large pup can push a toddler over,

Puppies are used to playing together in the litter, so they will enjoy games with their new human family.

creating in that child a serious and long-lasting fear of dogs. Sharp puppy teeth can easily puncture a baby's skin, unintentionally but still painfully. Small hands clutching a tiny puppy can really hurt, and a child who does not know how to pick up a puppy properly may drop it.

It's important that any dog be accustomed to being around children. If you do not have children of your own, register for a puppy class so that you have the chance of socializing your puppy with other pups and children under controlled conditions. If you have friends with children, ask them to visit and play with the pup. If your puppy is reluctant to go to children, do not force her. Take time, use plenty of praise and treats, and, until she is comfortable with children, make sure your puppy only meets children who are good with dogs.

If you have children of your own, teach them to respect the pup and not treat her as a toy to be picked up, carried about, and then dropped on the floor. Make sure the children learn to leave the pup alone when she is in her crate or when she is sleeping or eating.

PLAYING GAMES

Most children and pups get a lot of fun out of playing together, but their games should always be supervised. Avoid rough play since the puppy will get overexcited and the children may end up in tears. If a child hurts another child in play, the "victim" will usually retaliate by hitting back. The only way a dog can retaliate is with his teeth and the consequences of this can be disastrous.

Once the pup knows his name, hide-and-seek is a good game for the children to play with him. One child can hold the pup while the other runs and hides. When the "hider" calls the pup, the other child can let him go. After the pup is used to doing this, he can have his eyes hidden while the child hides, and he can start "searching" with his nose.

Tug-of-war games, especially with larger pups, are popular. (Note: Young children may need to "win" to avoid upsets.) Take the tug toy away when the game is finished. Many pups enjoy retrieving, and a ball can supply endless pleasure to both pups and children. Chasing games may be fun, but they are not always a good idea. Pups love chasing and being chased, but unless the pup is caught during the game, rewarded, and the game restarted, it is easy to end up with a pup who refuses to be caught.

This little girl is used to playing with a lively puppy, but supervision is essential so that the puppy does not become over-excited and frighten the child.

HELPING WITH TRAINING

Most children over the age of seven or eight can help with training. When it is time to feed the puppy, let the child call the pup and ask him to sit (see Chapter 5), and then reward him with his food. Children can also practice the "Down" command using a treat as a reward. But make sure this is not done too often—once or twice at a time is enough.

Older children can take the puppy out on a leash, although they should be accompanied by an adult.

Puppies and Babies

Often when a family brings home a new baby, there is a drastic shift in the amount and quality of attention they pay to their pets. Is it surprising then that the puppy, previously the center of attention, is a bit jealous of the new baby? Unfortunately, many owners don't understand this jealousy—if the pup shows any sign of resentment, he is accused of "turning nasty." The owners then treat the puppy harshly, which makes matters worse. This is not really the parents' fault, as they instinctively feel protective of the new arrival.

The best course of action is to introduce your puppy to some friends' babies before the arrival of yours. However, if that is not possible, try to make sure that the puppy is not left out of things—let him see that the baby is now part of the family, just as he is. Make a fuss over the puppy, too, so he knows that he is still loved.

If you are interested in some new object, you use your eyes. A puppy will also do this, but his nose is more important to him. So let the puppy sniff the baby—that does not mean lick the baby all over—in order to familiarize himself with the infant. If the puppy appears worried when the baby cries, try to ignore him or call him over and give him a treat. Never leave a dog of any age alone with a baby or young child.

Puppies and Other Pets

If you have a cat who is used to dogs already, it should not be a problem to add a new puppy to the household if you can prevent the puppy from chasing the cat. However, cats are unpredictable creatures and you cannot tell how a cat who is unaccustomed to dogs is going to react. Some will attack a small puppy such as a Yorkshire Terrier, while other cats go berserk, climbing up the curtains and spitting furiously. Fortunately, most family cats are tolerant creatures and common sense should be all that is needed for all to live in peace.

Your pup is almost certain to want to investigate this strange creature (unless she has been brought up with cats), so introduce them under controlled conditions in the house.

Put the pup on a collar and leash, and if the cat just sits and stares, or bristles slightly, let the pup approach gradually. If the cat decides to take off, stop the pup from chasing it, and try again.

Dogs and cats brought up together can become good friends.

Big dogs are often gentle with small puppies—but they should not be left alone together, as the bigger dog could be rough unintentionally with the smaller pet.

Never let the pup chase after the cat, yapping at it. Some cats will give a "nosy" pup a hefty swipe with a paw. If the pup is large and bouncy, it will do her no harm and will probably make her more respectful next time. However, if you have a small puppy, try not to let this happen since it could scare her or hurt her.

If you have pet rabbits or guinea pigs, they will probably be in hutches, cages, or outside runs, so they should be safe from small puppies—but do not let the pup run around yapping at them. Introduce the puppy quietly and check her with a firm "no" if she refuses to leave them alone. Find something else for the puppy to do, play ball with her, or give her a favorite toy. She should soon start accepting your small pets and lose interest, but never leave her alone with them.

A New Puppy and the Family Dog

Many people consider taking on a new puppy as the family dog enters old age. In this way the eventual loss of the older dog is often eased. However, you need to think carefully before going ahead with this.

Never bring in a young pup if you have a chronically sick old dog, or one that suffers from arthritis or a similar joint illness. The dog will not enjoy being bounced around by a youngster.

However, if you have an old dog who enjoys the company of other dogs, one who has slowed down and mellowed, then a puppy may give him a new lease on life. If you feel that your dog would benefit from the company of a puppy—and members of the family want one—then go ahead and buy one.

Introduce the pup and the old dog outside where there is more space and give them time to check each other over. You are, or should be, the pack leader, but the established dog will be dominant to the puppy —and the puppy will accept this. He is used to his mother being the boss dog and to taking his place in the litter with his siblings. He will expect the older dog to boss him about and so must you.

If, or more likely when, the old dog disciplines the puppy by turning him out of his bed, taking away a toy, giving a warning growl when he is eating or a quick snap when he wants to be left alone to sleep, you must not interfere and take the puppy's side. Leave them to sort it out; and unless you are very unlucky, they will soon settle into a satisfactory relationship.

Be careful to make the older dog feel loved and wanted when you introduce a new puppy to the family. In time they may become the best of friends.

If you have children, explain to them that both dogs need equal attention. Despite the obvious temptations, the puppy must not be fussed over to the exclusion of the old dog. Again, you must emphasize that the children must not interfere if the old dog gives the puppy a scolding. If they take the puppy's side against the old dog, there will almost certainly be more trouble between the dogs in the future.

The two dogs should not be together all the time. The old dog wants and deserves some peace in his old age and the puppy needs a chance to learn to be independent. You also want the puppy to enjoy interacting with the humans in the family, so make sure your puppy spends some time alone, and some one-on-one time with you or another member of the family.

The pup should sleep alone, and if the dogs are left at home for a while, the puppy should be put in a crate or in a different room. When the pup gets older and more mature, be prepared for him to take over as the dominant dog. This is quite natural and the old dog may well be relieved that someone younger is taking over the responsibility of guarding the family!

Puppies are inquisitive and enjoy discovering the outside world.

Puppies and Cars

Most dog owners like to take their dogs with them on a trip to the park, or even on a longer vacation. The sooner you start taking your pup in the car, the more likely he is to become accustomed to and enjoy traveling. Many pups are good travelers from the start, but quite a few will invariably suffer from car-sickness. If your puppy is prone to car-sickness, do not make the mistake of leaving him at home until he gets bigger. Chances are that the car-sickness will be worse if you wait.

Sedatives or anti-sickness pills can often help, so ask your vet to recommend something suitable for your puppy's age and size. However, do not rely on using pills for every outing. The best solution is to accustom your puppy to the car, and over a period of time he should become an excellent traveler.

You must decide where you want your puppy to ride in the car, bearing in mind that many dogs travel better when they cannot see out of the window. The pup can travel in a crate or a dog box. Some well-behaved pups enjoy traveling in the passenger foot-well. Recently, car seat belts for dogs have become available, though they are probably more suitable for older dogs.

Please do not let your puppy or grown dog ride behind a dog-guard in a small space at the back of the car. This area has not become known as the "crumple zone" for nothing. If the puppy gets worried, sick, or starts barking, you will not be able to do anything to help him until you are able to stop the car and get out. This area can also get very hot for the dog.

THE PERILS OF HOT CARS

Cars in the sun can quickly turn into ovens, and many dogs have died of heat stroke and dehydration when left in parked cars. Even on a cool day, the oxygen inside a closed car quickly gets used up. It is absolutely essential to have adequate ventilation in any parked car with a dog inside.

Do not feed the puppy right before you start on a journey and make sure you give him a chance to relieve himself before getting into the car. Put him on a collar and leash, and for long journeys take along a friend (one who likes puppies—even messy ones). Make sure you take an old towel and some newspapers, just in case. If the pup is sick, do not make a fuss, just clean him up and, as soon as you can, stop the car and let him out for a short run. This is often enough to settle a pup so that he can finish the ride without further problems.

Puppies, like children, need patience—and frequent bathroom breaks!

Make sure you keep the puppy quiet in the car. If you have young children in the car, make it a rule that they do not play with the pup when traveling. It is a good idea to give him a toy or nylon bone to chew. Start with short trips and frequent stops. Try to go to a place where the puppy can run free, such as the local park. Let him out for a short run and then go on a little farther and let him out again. Make the journeys fun! The puppy will not learn to enjoy the car if all he ever does is go to the vet.

Once your puppy is happy about traveling, teach him to get in the car on his own (unless he is too small to jump in). Start with the pup sitting outside the door, then get in the car yourself and call him, encouraging him with a treat. Once the puppy is willing to do this, ask your puppy to sit; then throw a treat into the car and tell him to "get in." Praise him well when he responds. Never let your puppy get into the car until you say so, and never let him jump out until he is told. Get out of the car yourself, telling the pup to stay. If he tries to rush out, either push him back or hold him back with the leash. Wait until he has settled, then tell him "OK" and let him out, praising well. This is very important—dogs have been run over or have caused accidents by jumping out of cars unexpectedly.

The final lesson is to teach your puppy to stay in the car on his own. If you have taught him to stay alone at home, this should not pose a problem. More likely, the problem will be with other people coming over to admire the "cute puppy," or holding their own dog up to the window to say hello—not to mention the ones who will come over and say "woof" in the hope that your puppy will answer them—as he undoubtedly will!

If you have a small puppy, it is best to leave him in a traveling box where he cannot be seen. When you first leave the pup, go a short distance away, just out of sight. If he does not bark after a minute or two, go back and praise him and give him a treat. If he does bark, go back and bang loudly on the roof of the car, growling "no." This almost always works. Once the pup is quiet, leave him again and if he barks again, do the same thing. If he is quiet, go back and praise him. Only leave him for a very short time to begin with and gradually increase it. You may have to work on this for quite a while, but it is well worth the effort to have a puppy who can be safely left on his own, knowing that he will behave. Remember, of course, that cars heat up very quickly on warm days and your pet can suffer greatly in a very short time if left alone in a hot car.

House Rules

Decide early on what the rules are going to be and enforce them consistently. For example, your puppy may greet you with jumping every time you walk through the door. It's easy for you to respond with a show of affection. However, if you get mad at your puppy one day when she jumps on you with muddy paws, she will be confused.

All pups like to jump up; it is a natural action. They jump up at their mother to suckle and they jump all over their siblings in play. However, you need to

It's important to teach your puppy the "house rules" so that he knows what is allowed and what is not acceptable.

teach your pet that jumping on people is unacceptable, especially if she is going to be a large adult! Sometimes it is enough to ignore your puppy when she jumps up, but make sure the rest of the family reacts in the same way. After a while, the pup should think it not worth jumping up if no one takes any notice.

However, most pups are persistent and you will have to do a bit more to stop this behavior. Your object should be to teach the dog that you make a fuss of her when she is sitting—not when she is jumping up. In this instance, do not use the command "Down," since this should only mean "lie down on the floor." Instead, growl at your puppy (like her mother did when she was in the nest), push her down, and give the command "Sit." Once the puppy is sitting, praise her quietly. If you make too much fuss, she will start all over again.

If you see that the puppy is about to jump, tell her to sit. With consistent attention to this, she will soon abandon the idea of jumping up on

people. In the meantime, do not allow your children to start shouting, "get down," "stop it," etc. This will just make the puppy over-excited and will encourage her to bounce about even more. If you have not been firm enough with your puppy and she persists in jumping up, try holding her paws, if she is a large puppy, until she climbs down.

Consistency is essential. Do not allow your puppy to sit on the sofa on one occasion and then yell at him the next time he does it.

28

When a visitor comes to the door, put your puppy on her leash and tell her to sit. Keep her in this position until the friend comes in. Ask the friend to gently stroke the puppy, and then let her free. If you want to impress your friends, teach your pup to shake hands. Most dogs (and visitors) enjoy this routine.

Once the puppy has learned her name, which she should always associate with pleasure, she must next learn "No" and "OK." No means "stop what you are doing now," and OK means just that. Do not shout at your puppy—she hears much better than you do. Growl out your "No" and praise her in a happy voice.

Neither dogs nor puppies should go through doors or gates before you, or any other member of the family. The behaviorists emphasize that this is to show your dominance over the pup, but it also has a practical purpose. Puppies rushing through open doors can knock toddlers down, cause old people to fall, and trip up anyone in their way. A puppy which rushes out of the door could run into the road and get knocked down by a car. So this is a useful rule for everyone's benefit.

When the situation first arises, simply say "No" and use your hand to hold the puppy back. Once you are through the door, tell him "OK" and pat him when he comes to you. As soon as you have taught your puppy to sit, tell him to sit before you open the door; then use a hand signal to help keep him there. Once you are through the door, tell him "OK" and call him. Do not make too much fuss of him or he will get over-excited.

3

CARING FOR YOUR PUPPY

Feeding

Young pups need three or four times the energy intake of an adult of the same breed in order to allow for growth and their high activity level. Like human babies, puppies have small stomachs and therefore need several small meals a day. At eight weeks of age, four meals a day are sufficient, gradually decreasing to one or two meals per day when adult. Small and toy breeds mature early, usually around six to nine months, but large and giant breeds may not reach adult weight until eighteen or even twenty-four months.

Young puppies expend an enormous amount of energy, so it is essential to feed them a nutritious, well-balanced diet.

CHOOSING A DIET

Keep to the diet the pup is used to for the first few days after you bring him home. If you want to change the diet, do so gradually. There is a huge variety of puppy foods on the market and those made by reputable firms are usually very good. You can take your pick from canned meat and/or dry food in a number of forms. What really matters is that the pup is fed a balanced diet, enjoys his food and thrives on it. The occasional serving of "human" foods won't hurt your puppy either, such as finely chopped meat, cheese, bread, or cooked eggs.

SUPPLEMENTS

Do not be tempted by all the advertisements for minerals, vitamins and other supplements. If you are feeding a balanced diet, this is sufficient for your puppy's dietary needs. Adding supplements can provide too much of some nutrients, doing more harm than good, so consult your vet before using any of these.

GOOD MANNERS AT PUPPY MEALTIMES

Although a pup should be left in peace to eat his food, he must be taught to accept the fact that you, or any of the family, have the right to go up to him when he is eating, or even remove his food if you wish. Start off by telling your puppy to sit when you put down his food bowl, then tell him he can eat. While he is eating, stroke him gently and talk to him. Most pups will be so busy eating, they will not even notice. But if your puppy does growl at you, immediately growl back, grasp him by the scruff of his neck and make him sit. Once he has calmed down, let him start eating again and stroke him. If your puppy is behaving well, drop a treat into his bowl to show him that you did not really want his dinner. Keep repeating this at different times until your puppy accepts the stroking, then tell him to sit and remove his bowl. When the puppy accepts this, offer him a treat. In a short time most pups look forward to the bowl being removed and refilled with tasty bits.

If you have children, this lesson is very important. The day will come when one of them will run up when your puppy is eating, bounce a ball near him, or make a grab at the food bowl. If the puppy has not been taught to accept having his food removed, there could be a nasty accident.

WATER

A dog can go without food for several days, losing 40% of his body weight without dying; but with water loss of only 10–15% he can die. Your puppy must have access to clean water all the time, especially if he is fed a dry diet. The exception to this is at night. You cannot expect a small pup to be dry at night if he has a large drink at 2:00 A.M.

MEAL TIMES

Wild dogs and wolves eat only when they manage to catch their dinner. Their puppies, once weaned, get a meal only when a member of the pack brings it to them, which is certainly not on a regular schedule of four feedings a day. So you don't have to worry if you can't stick to feeding times that are exactly the same from day to day. It won't harm the puppy to eat a little earlier or a little later.

Feed on your schedule and don't fall into the habit of feeding the puppy whenever he asks for it. The last meal of the day should be a few hours before bedtime so the puppy has time to digest it before sleeping, which also lessens the likelihood of needing to relieve himself during the night. Never feed your puppy before a car trip or before vigorous exercise.

Remember that treats add up—especially for toy breeds. A handful of treats to a small dog is more like a meal for him. Be careful not to overfeed.

PROBLEM FEEDERS

If a healthy puppy refuses his dinner but begs you for something else to eat, he is usually just testing you. Do not give in to him. If your puppy leaves his food, just take the bowl away and offer him fresh food at the next mealtime. However, if your pup refuses his food and acts like he might be getting sick, you should consult your vet.

Exercise and Rest

All puppies—and all dogs of whatever age, size, or breed—need exercise. They also need to play; and very often the two can be happily combined. However, do not force a puppy to go on if she seems to be getting tired. Do not try to make your puppy jump over awkward or high obstacles until she is at least six or even nine months old.

Puppies also need their rest time to wind down and allow their bodies to recharge and grow. Remember that your bouncy, active puppy still requires naps!

Rest is an important part of development. Puppies appreciate plenty of time to sleep without being disturbed.

Grooming

Grooming is an important part of canine life. Wild dogs groom each other in an act of friendship and this helps cement the pack together. In a domestic situation, the grooming session should be an enjoyable time, one that strengthens the bond between puppy and owner.

Most puppies do not require much grooming, but don't make the mistake of assuming they need no grooming at all. If you have a short-coated breed you may feel it is not worth bothering to groom him. This is definitely not the case. All puppies need to be handled and you cannot start this too soon. It will be time well spent, and a vet or show judge will appreciate a dog who behaves sensibly and allows itself to be handled without any fuss.

Quietly coax the pup to sit still while you run your hands over him, open his mouth, pick up his feet, and look in his ears. Rub his tummy if you like—the object of the exercise is for the puppy to enjoy being groomed. If your puppy wriggles, hold him until he relaxes, then praise him or give him a treat.

Start early to help your puppy get used to being handled and groomed.

Once the puppy accepts being handled, place him on a table, and start brushing him, making sure you use a good-quality bristle brush. The pup can be sitting, standing, or lying down. If you have a long-coated breed, grooming is easier if the dog learns to lie flat. If the pup already knows how to lie down, give him a command such as "flat," and gently roll him on his side, keeping him there for a few seconds.

Once the puppy is relaxed, praise him and let him get up again. Be firm, but do not have a fight. As soon as your puppy is lying quietly, you can start brushing him.

Most breeds need only a few minutes of daily grooming and a more thorough grooming once a week. On the other hand, if you have an Old English Sheepdog, Afghan Hound, or a Pekingese, grooming will be much more time-consuming.

The Perfect Finish for Any Type of Coat

SMOOTH-COATED: A grooming glove is very useful for dogs with smooth coats. The gloves usually have short, rubber teeth on one side, and corduroy or velvet on the other side. Use the rubber side to remove dead hairs and the other side for massaging and "polishing."

LONG-COATED: Using a steel comb, gently comb out the hair, with careful attention to areas behind the ears and under the armpits where mats are likely to form. Knots or tangles should be gently worked out—never tug on chunks of hair with the comb. Brush a small amount of coat at a time, making sure the bristles go right down to the skin, and work over the whole animal.

WIRE-HAIRED: Wire-haired dogs, like Wire Fox Terriers, have coarse outer coats and dense, soft undercoats. They need regular grooming with a "stripping knife," which looks like a penknife with serrated edges. Ask the puppy's breeder or your local pet store for advice on the proper way to groom him or buy a book about the breed. Brush the coat regularly between trims.

STIFF/STAND-OFF: Breeds with stiff, stand-off coats, such as some of the Spitz breeds, Chow Chows, Keeshonds, etc., should first have their coats brushed against the growth of the hair and then carefully brushed back into place. You may want to buy a special "rake" tool to remove the large amount of hair that loosens when these breeds shed.

NON-SHEDDING: Poodles, and a few other breeds, do not shed their coats (which is a great help to any dog lover who suffers from asthma). This type of coat keeps on growing, and, unless it is properly looked after. it can end up in a matted mess. Most poodle owners use the service of a grooming parlor on a regular basis, although you can learn to do the grooming yourself.

Poodles do not shed their coats, so many owners enlist the services of a professional groomer to keep the coat in shape.

NAILS

In the wild, canines wear their nails down naturally. However, most dogs kept as companions need to have their nails cut and/or filed regularly. Get your puppy used to having his feet handled. Make a game of it, rolling the pup over and catching hold of his feet. When the puppy accepts this, you can progress until the pup will lie still and allow you to examine his feet. Do not forget to reward the puppy when he does what you want.

When a dog is standing naturally, his nails should just touch the ground. If the nails are too long it makes walking uncomfortable. The nails tend to split and often the feet splay out. A puppy with long nails is also likely to cause you some painful scratches, however unintentionally.

Your puppy's nails may not need much attention at first, but it is a good practice to keep the tips snipped off. Buy some strong, good-quality nail clippers. A coarse file can be used to smooth rough edges. Some puppies that strongly resist the nail clippers will sit quite calmly while you use a file instead.

Light-colored nails are easier to clip than dark ones, because the quick (the blood supply) is easily seen as a thin, pink line down the middle of the nail. Be careful never to cut the quick: it is extremely painful, bleeds profusely, and the experience may make your puppy resist future nail trims.

If your puppy has both light and dark nails, cut the light ones first. This will give you a better idea of how much to take off the dark nails where you cannot see the quick. If in doubt, it is usually safe to trim off the tip of the nail at the point where it starts to turn down. It is often easier to see where to cut a nail by turning the foot up and cutting from underneath the pad. If your puppy has dewclaws (usually located on the inside of the front legs, occasionally on the inside of back legs too), these must be checked regularly. They do not wear down naturally and, if neglected, they can grow right into the leg, causing nasty abscesses and a lot of unnecessary pain.

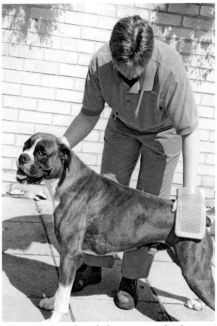

A grooming glove helps remove dead hairs and polish the coat.

TEETH

Puppies have a set of twenty-eight "baby" teeth, which, as you will soon discover, are sharp! Between four and seven months, the permanent teeth (averaging forty-two in number) come through, starting with the incisors and ending with the molars.

Unlike human babies, puppies rarely have teething troubles, but teething can cause a certain amount of stress, and puppies often become more sensitive to their environment during the teething period.

At this time be careful how you handle your pup, especially around his mouth. When a puppy is teething, he must chew in order to loosen his baby teeth and make way for the adult teeth. Make sure your puppy has plenty of hard nylon or rubber toys to gnaw on.

In most cases, the baby teeth come out on their own, but in some of the smaller breeds, they are retained as the new ones come in. Keep checking to see if the teeth are coming loose, and if they do not appear to be moving, consult your vet—the baby teeth may need to be extracted.

Dogs, like most people, eventually develop tartar on their teeth. If you keep the teeth in good condition while the dog is still young, it can help prevent tartar forming. Even if the puppy has finished teething, make sure he has hard nylon or rubber toys, hard dog biscuits and marrow bones to chew on.

Most vets advise cleaning a dog's teeth about once a week. There are various canine toothpastes and toothbrushes on the market, but you can do a good job with a gauze pad (or an ordinary toothbrush) soaked in saline solution or baking soda and water. Rub this around the teeth vigorously. The inner surfaces of the teeth are usually kept clean by the dog's tongue.

Bathing

Get your puppy used to having a bath while he is still fairly young and small enough to be manageable. The goal is to make it fun. Never fight with a struggling pup and make a big issue of it. If possible, choose a dry, sunny day. You will need a good-quality dog shampoo. (Do not use your shampoo or dishwashing liquid.) If you suspect your puppy has fleas, insecticidal shampoos are available to treat these stubborn pests.

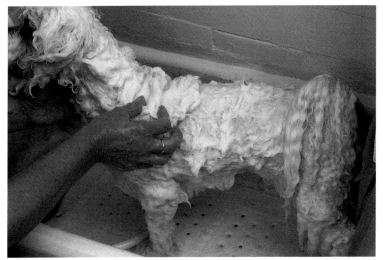

If you make bathing a fun and enjoyable experience when your puppy is small, you'll save yourself many battles later!

Depending on the size of your puppy you can use the sink, the shower, or a tub. Use a non-slip rubber mat to give the puppy secure footing. The water should be warm, and should come up no higher than the puppy's tummy. Lift the pup carefully into the water and wet him thoroughly with a sprayer attachment. Apply shampoo, working it into a good lather. Leave the puppy's head until last, otherwise when his head is wet he will want to shake and you will be left soaking wet with the pup only half-washed! Don't get shampoo into his eyes or ears. If you are worried about getting water or shampoo in his ears, put some cotton in them (some puppies will simply shake this out but it's worth a try).

Once your puppy is clean, rinse him thoroughly with tepid water. A hose or hand-held shower attachment makes the job easier. When you have rinsed out all the shampoo, slip a leash on your puppy, lift him out of the water and let him have a good shake. Dry him off thoroughly so he doesn't get cold afterward. Give him a good rub with a terry-cloth towel and, if it is sunny outside, either take him for a walk or let him play in the yard while he finishes drying.

TAKE CARE OF YOUR TOOLS
Always keep your grooming equipment clean—it is not much use grooming a dog with a dirty brush.

Give your puppy a "check-up" once a week as part of your grooming routine. He will soon get used to you doing this...

...and you will be more likely to catch health problems at an early stage.

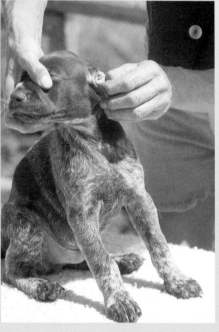

If your pup is a long-coated breed such as an Afghan Hound, a Rough Collie, or a Bearded Collie, it is better to dry him with a hair dryer. If you attempt to towel-dry this type of coat, the hair may tangle or break. You'll need to get the pup used to the hair dryer and may want to do this before you actually give him a bath. Have the puppy lie on the floor or your lap while you talk to him and play with one of his toys in one hand. Hold the dryer in your other hand and put it on at a low setting, gradually bringing it nearer the puppy until he accepts it.

Weekly Health Checks

With luck and proper care, your puppy should need little in the way of medical attention during the first year. Once a week, do a thorough grooming and take time to check the following:

- Are the eyes bright and clear? Eyes are very delicate and can easily be harmed, so take the puppy to the vet if you suspect a problem.

- Check the nose: is it clear and free from discharge? If the dog's nose is cracked or raw, a smear of olive oil, petroleum jelly, or cod liver oil will help. The puppy will lick most of it off, but what is left will do some good.

- Open the mouth and check the teeth and gums. Gums should be healthy and pink in color, although some breeds have black or black-spotted gums. Once your puppy starts teething, check the mouth quite frequently to make sure the second teeth are coming in correctly.

- Check the ears. If an ear is foul-smelling or has an unpleasant discharge, seek veterinary advice. Never poke anything into an ear. However, you can easily clean off any normal dirt or wax with a piece of damp cotton. In the summer, watch out for burr-like grass seeds which can get stuck in hair and cause problems in breeds with long, silky-coated ears, such as spaniels.

- Check the foot pads for cuts or cracks and see if the nails need to be trimmed. Look between and under the pads, too, since some long-haired breeds get mats in between the toes. If these are not cut out they can cause lameness and sore feet. The best way to do this is with a pair of blunt-nosed, curved scissors.

- If you have a male puppy, check the penis and sheath. In a puppy or young dog any slight discharge should be light and clear. If there is a smelly or discolored discharge, consult your vet. Most male dogs leave drops of urine scattered around underneath when they urinate. In long-haired breeds this tends to make the hairs round the sheath sticky and rather unpleasant, so keep the hair short in this area and give it an occasional wash.

Vaccination

Puppies are now usually vaccinated against distemper, hepatitis, and parvovirus. Leptospirosis may be indicated for dogs in your area and rabies vaccinations are usually required by law. Dogs that will stay in boarding kennels or attend dog shows may also need to vaccinated against "kennel cough" (bordetella). Consult your vet to see which vaccinations are appropriate for your puppy.

Most vets begin the vaccination series when the puppy is 6–8 weeks of age. Your puppy may have had his first injection before leaving the breeder, in which case he will have to go to the vet to finish the course. After the course is finished, your dog will need periodic booster shots. Your vet will recommend a schedule for these.

Vaccinations and other preventive health programs, such as worming, should begin during the puppy stage and continue throughout the dog's life.

Internal Parasites

ROUNDWORMS

Virtually all puppies have roundworms called Toxocara Canis. Although pups can have worms without any telltale signs in their feces, roundworms can often be seen as whitish-colored thread-like objects, usually from 2–8 inches (5–20 cms) long. Worms can cause vomiting and diarrhea in dogs, but have serious health risks for humans (Toxocara Canis can cause blindness but fortunately this is extremely rare). If your puppy is wormed regularly there will be no danger to your family.

Most vets recommend worming for roundworms in puppies at two, four, six, eight, and twelve weeks. Many of today's worming preparations can be fed to the puppy with his normal meal. In fact, some wormers are now incorporated into the food. Although many worming products can be bought "over the counter," it's best to ask your vet for advice to ensure you have a safe, effective remedy. In most cases, dogs should be wormed routinely every six months and at any other time the owner suspects worm infestation.

There are other worms which affect dogs, tapeworms being the most common. Heartworms can affect dogs living in some parts of the United States, particularly the southeastern coastal areas. Your vet can test your puppy and put him on a preventative medication.

External Parasites

FLEAS

Even the best-cared-for puppy can pick up fleas, especially if he comes into regular contact with other dogs. Fleas are worst during warm weather. Regular grooming will help to keep your dog free from fleas, but you will also need to use some other preventative measure, such as a flea collar, anti-parasitic flea spray, or a topical preparation available from your vet.

If your puppy is scratching, look for evidence of flea infestation. You may not see the fleas themselves, but you may see "flea-dirt"—black grain-like droppings. For puppies under twelve weeks old, do not use flea treatments without a vet's advice. Instead, use a fine-toothed "flea comb" to remove the pests. Older puppies can be bathed with an insecticidal shampoo. Fleas can live in carpets and on bedding, so you must treat the puppy's bedding as well as carpets, furniture, etc.

TICKS

Ticks are parasites that suck at the dog's blood until they become bloated. Do not be tempted to try to pull the tick from your puppy, as this will leave the mouthpiece firmly implanted in the dog's skin. The best treatment is to apply a mild antiseptic using a cotton ball to get the tick to release its hold. Ticks can spread a variety of diseases so it is important to monitor for them, especially if your dog spends a lot of time outdoors. If you live in an area with a high incidence of tick-borne Lyme disease, ask your vet about the vaccine to prevent this.

DIARRHEA

The most common health problem a puppy is likely to suffer in the first twelve months of its life is diarrhea. The puppy may have eaten too much, he may have reacted to a change of diet, or he may have picked up a bacterial or viral illness. The best course of action is to withhold food for a twenty-four hour period, making sure that fresh, clean drinking water is readily available. When you next feed your puppy, give him something plain and easy to digest such as chicken or fish and rice. In most cases this will solve the problem. If the condition persists, ask your vet for advice. If you ever see signs of blood in the stools, contact your vet immediately.

UNDERSTANDING YOUR PUPPY

How Dogs Learn

Dogs learn by association of ideas, as do all the higher animals. This simply means that if an animal does something either accidentally or by persuasion and finds it pleasant, he will tend to do it again. If it is unpleasant or frightening, he will be reluctant to do it again.

The first step in training is to get the dog's attention.

CORRECTION AND REWARD

In order to get the dog to do what you want, and just as important, to refrain from doing what you do not want, you must build up desirable association of ideas by a process of correction and reward. Correction could be described as any action which prevents the dog from doing what he intends, or persuades him to do what the trainer wants him to do—such as pushing him into a sitting position.

Only the minimum of correction should ever be used, and when the dog responds, no matter how reluctantly, he should be immediately rewarded. It is easy to over-correct, but it is very difficult to over-reward. Correction or reward must be applied as the action takes place, or within seconds of it taking place, otherwise the dog will not know what experience is being corrected or rewarded.

STRENGTH OF ASSOCIATIONS

The strongest and most lasting associations are those created by fear. Following this are the first-time associations and experiences which happen over and over again. If a puppy is frightened by the first dog she meets, the effect will be far greater than if she had previously met friendly dogs. Another point to remember is that the effect of frightening experiences increases as the puppy gets older. A sixteen-week-old puppy may be absolutely terrified of something which may not have affected her when she was seven weeks old.

A threatened animal can adopt one of three options: fight, flight, or freeze. However, it is rare for a young puppy to fight, no matter the provocation. The pup will either freeze by becoming submissive—probably rolling on her back and waving her paws in the air—or she will flee.

Flight is actually the biggest danger, and not just because the puppy may run into the path of traffic. The farther she runs, the greater her separation from you, her protector. Like a lost child, she panics and becomes even more terrified. Just a single experience like this can change the puppy's personality. The most likely result is that the puppy will be afraid of strange dogs, or she may only be afraid of the type of dog which frightened her. Additionally, the puppy may associate the fright with the place, and she may be afraid of going near the spot where the incident took place, even when there is no dog there. If the puppy gets chased by a dog on several occasions, she may be apprehensive about going out for a walk at all.

Relating to Other Dogs

It goes against the laws of nature for an adult dog to attack a submissive puppy and it is very rare to find one that does. But it is natural for any dog to chase anything which runs away, whether it is a child, a sheep, a puppy, or a ball rolling along the ground. When you take your puppy out in a public open space, you should always assume that the dogs you meet are not under control. Most of them will be, but a false assumption can lead to big trouble.

If a strange dog comes bounding up, do not worry about whether or not he is friendly and certainly do not listen to the owner's assurance to that effect. Just put your puppy on a leash so he does not run away. Do not drag the pup away from the other dog, do not scream at him "come here," and do not pick him up. In short, do not do anything that might give the puppy the impression that there is anything to be frightened of. If the strange dog proves to be friendly, allow him to sniff the puppy, but do not touch either of them while this is taking place.

Instinct and Intelligence

To the vast majority of owners, the outstanding feature of any dog, especially their own, is his intelligence. But, in fact, the reason why the dog has become such a valuable servant and friend to mankind is because of his instincts. Most dogs are sufficiently intelligent to be able to learn anything we want to teach them, provided the right instincts are there.

Instinct makes an animal do something without any learning. First comes the instinct to survive, which makes the newborn puppy squirm around until he finds a teat and then starts sucking. As he grows up, other instincts will develop. These will vary according to the breed, and they will also vary in strength between individuals of the same breed.

SIGN UP FOR PUPPY CLASSES
At puppy classes, puppies meet other dogs in a controlled environment. They also learn to mix with strangers, both adults and children, and to discover that this can be fun, usually ending with a tasty treat. The puppy learns the body language of his kind, which teaches him how to react to different dogs in different situations, and, above all, never to run away when he sees a strange dog.

The Border Collie usually has an exceptionally strong herding instinct. While this is an asset for farm dogs, it is something that pet owners will have to channel into more appropriate behaviors.

Every owner should make an effort to understand the instincts which are present in their dog. Whether it is an asset or a liability, an instinct can be controlled by training and by diverting it into other channels. If it is to be an asset, it should be encouraged as soon as it makes an appearance. If it is likely to be a liability, you must be ready to control it the very first time it shows.

All breeds have inherited some hunting instinct from the wolf. With selective breeding, man has strengthened this instinct in some breeds. The wolf only hunts when it is hungry, but many breeds of dog will hunt just for the sake of hunting. Man has also modified the hunting instinct to develop instincts which he can use to his own advantage. The best examples of these are the herding and retrieving instincts.

THE HERDING INSTINCT
Contrary to common belief, it is not because of its superior intelligence that the Border Collie reigns supreme as a sheep dog—it is because of the breed's instinct to herd. The average Labrador Retriever is just as intelligent as the average Border Collie, but a Labrador will not work sheep because it has no herding instinct. However, the Labrador will usually retrieve instinctively, whereas other breeds have to be taught to do this.

The herding instinct in the modern Border Collie is often over-developed. As a pet, this sort of dog will herd anything from the neighbor's cat to a city bus. This exceptionally strong herding instinct is very often accompanied by an abundance of initiative and energy. If given nothing to do, the dog will be extremely frustrated and may become unmanageable.

Instincts strengthen with use. If a pup is not allowed to use an instinct, that instinct will usually become weaker and perhaps die out completely.

THE RETRIEVING INSTINCT
Other breeds have instincts which have been developed by man for various purposes, and this includes the retrievers and most spaniel breeds. Dogs like these usually pick up objects and carry them around without any training, although the age at which they start showing this instinct varies.

Labrador and Golden Retrievers were bred to be superb retrievers. Most of these puppies will pick up any object and carry it around without any encouragement or training.

All dogs enjoy having something to do and many dogs get into trouble because they are "unemployed." One way to overcome this is to make use of the instincts which your particular type of dog has inherited. If you have a spaniel or retriever pup, encourage him to bring your slippers, pick up the mail, etc. He will be far happier using his instincts than sitting idly at home in the yard, or worse, digging it up through frustration.

THE HUNTING INSTINCT

Hound puppies frequently have an even stronger hunting instinct than the wild dog. They can be divided into two groups: sighthounds who hunt by sight, and scenthounds who hunt by using their noses. Sighthounds include such breeds as Afghans, Salukis, Greyhounds, and Whippets. They disprove the widely held belief that dogs have poor eyesight compared with humans.

A Greyhound can spot a moving hare half a mile away, before the average human can see it.

Scenthounds do not bother to look—they simply put their noses down and follow the track of their quarry. Beagles and Basset Hounds, both popular as pets, are well-known members of this group.

Sighthounds have a highly refined chasing instinct which makes them great at racing, but not always suitable as pets.

THE GUARDING INSTINCT

Most people like to think that their dog would protect them if the occasion arose, and in fact the majority of all breeds (including crossbreeds and mongrels) will attempt to do so.

Some breeds, such as the Rottweiler, German Shepherd, and Doberman Pinscher, have been bred specifically to have a stronger than average guarding instinct. Instead of waiting for something to happen, they tend to anticipate the danger and take action to prevent it happening. A dog of this type needs experienced handling.

There are also some breeds that are classed as Sheepdogs but do not herd in the same way as the Border Collie. They have been bred to stay with the flock and guard it against all predators, two-legged or four-legged. Maremma Sheepdogs and Great Pyrenees are in this category.

THE TERRIER BREEDS

The enormous range of terriers have all been bred to kill vermin, such as rats and rabbits; so terriers were expected to be tough and active, with a strong killing instinct. Today they are known for their determined and spirited personalities, and they may not be the best choice for homes with small children or other pets since terriers like to be in charge.

The German Shepherd, one of the guarding breeds, is used as a police dog worldwide.

The terrier breeds are tough, active, and full of character.

5

TRAINING YOUR PUPPY

Different people want their pups to learn different things, but it is fairly safe to say that most people want a dog who is clean in the house, walks quietly on a leash, sits and lies down on command, and comes when called.

The Recall

Before tackling this exercise, let us first solve the problem of why so many dogs refuse to come when called. The answer is that their owners have (unintentionally) taught them not to respond.

Training cannot start too early. These puppies are already running to the sound they associate with food. This is the beginning of teaching the "Recall."

This puppy is being rewarded for coming when she was called.

It happens in many ways, such as calling the puppy, and then shouting at him when he does not come immediately. But as far as the pup is concerned, he has been scolded for coming—since that was the last thing he did. So, bearing this in mind, always attract your pup's attention before you call him. Always call him in a happy, cheerful voice and praise him when he comes to you.

Dogs understand sounds, not words, and they associate certain sounds with certain actions. One of the first, if not the first, association which any puppy should learn is that if he responds to his name he will be rewarded. However, do not use food as the reward every time. Your goal is to have a dog who obeys whether you have food or not. If he is only given food at odd intervals, he will not come to regard it as a right.

It is much easier to teach a puppy to stay with you before his hunting and other instincts have fully developed. There is also a submissive instinct which makes the pup want to please you, and cultivating that instinct is part of the training process.

We are often told of the importance of preventing bad habits in our pets, but seldom of the importance of developing good ones. If a puppy strays too far from you, but is recalled and immediately rewarded every time he comes to you, he should soon develop the habit of staying within range. A good way of encouraging a pup to keep an eye on you is to hide behind a tree or bush when he is not looking. Keep the puppy in sight to make sure that he doesn't panic and run in the wrong direction when he notices you're gone. If he does, you will have to call him, but otherwise let him find you. Most puppies will quickly do this, using their noses.

Leash (Lead) Training

Many pups do not mind at all when a collar is first put on, but others scratch and generally protest for quite a while. Just ignore all the drama; the pup will accept the collar in time. Make sure you use a light, soft collar; it should not be too tight, nor so slack that the pup can get it off or get her jaw caught in it. Always take the collar off at night.

Do not start leash training (also called lead training) until your puppy will follow you without being on a leash (or lead). The leash is not something to make a dog go with the owner—it is a safety line to prevent her running away, and a means of controlling her when she is learning new exercises. If your pup struggles when you first put the leash on her, do not fight with her or drag her after you. Stand still, and as soon as the puppy relaxes, make a great fuss of her and encourage her with food to come up to you. Walk on a little way, holding a treat in your hand, and the puppy will want to follow you.

If the pup pulls against the leash, give her a sharp jerk, but not a hefty one that throws her head-over-heels. Once she has stopped, call her back to you, praise her well and start off again. You can also try standing still as soon as the puppy starts pulling. It takes two to pull, and the pup will not get any fun out of it if you will not "play." Once the puppy is behaving, praise her and start walking again, talking to her and trying to keep her attention. Make it fun! It is important that the pup look forward to going for a walk on the leash.

Start leash training your puppy early on. Food can be used to encourage the puppy to walk in the same direction as the owner.

The Sit

Teach the "Sit" command before the "Down." Call your puppy to you and when you have his attention, hold your hand just above his head, at the same time saying "Sit." As the pup looks up, move your hand toward the back of his head. His eyes should follow your hand movements, and he should automatically sit. As soon as he sits, give him a treat and praise him, but not too enthusiastically or he may get too excited to listen to you.

If the puppy shows signs of moving, place your hand on his rump to keep him still for a few seconds. Then tell him "OK" and let him get up. Repeat this four or five times, but stop before he gets bored or frustrated. When you have finished the lesson, have a game together.

Teach the "Sit" command before the "Down" command.

The Down

Once your puppy knows how to sit on command, you can start teaching him the "Down." First, command your puppy to sit and attract his attention. Hold your hand, with a treat in it, in front of the pup's head. Say "Down" and lower your hand to the ground just in front of him. As he goes down, praise him and give him the treat. Place your other hand on the puppy's shoulders to keep him there a moment before letting him up. If he is reluctant about going down, use your other hand from the start to press down on his shoulders.

When your puppy is sitting, attract his attention with a treat and then lower your hand, giving the command "Down."

Play Training

Once your puppy has mastered the basic exercises, you may wish to teach him some play exercises. This will be fun for you and your family—and results in a happier dog who receives plenty of stimulation and is eager to respond to his owner.

SHAKING HANDS

Perhaps the simplest trick of all is shaking hands. In fact, some dogs do it without ever being taught. Puppies instinctively knead at their mother's teats to stimulate the milk flow. Once the pups are older, the mother often stands up in response to this kneading and prodding. The pups then usually sit underneath her and suckle while reaching up with their paws. Giving a paw to "shake hands" is an extension of this natural action.

If your pup is the sort who offers up a paw, take it and reward him with a treat, giving him a command at the same time. If your puppy is not a "natural," you may have to start by giving a command and tapping his leg until he lifts it. When he responds, reward him. Be warned: some dogs become obsessed with shaking hands and try to do it all the time. Train your puppy to only do it when asked—and then to stop.

Puppies naturally use their paws when they are suckling from their mother. This instinct can be useful when teaching a pup to shake hands.

SIT UP AND BEG

This is something which should not be taught too soon since it can strain the back of an immature pup, especially one of a long-legged breed. However, as with shaking hands, some pups teach themselves. Small dogs take to begging easily. Have him sit; then hold a treat just above his head, command "Beg," and encourage him to sit up.

If this does not work, take the puppy to a corner which will support his back as he sits up. Say "Sit," hold his front paws in one hand, and say "Beg" while you hold a treat over his head with the other hand. Then gently lift his front paws up until he is in the right position. Make sure he is properly balanced. Once the puppy starts to go up on his own, be ready to support him if he loses his balance. Some dogs learn this quickly but others will need more time and patience.

CATCHING

This trick makes it easy to reward a dog immediately when he does what is wanted. A lot of dogs are natural catchers; others fail to see the point at all. It is best to start with food. Call the pup to you, stand a little way back, tell him to "Catch," making sure he is watching your hand, and throw or half-drop the treat toward his mouth.

If your puppy misses, pick up the treat, do not let him have it, and try again. If he manages to catch it, stop and start again the next day. As your puppy improves, gradually stand farther back until he can catch it from quite a distance. Once he is catching well, he can be taught to catch a ball (make sure it is large enough so that he cannot swallow it) or a Frisbee.

SPEAK ON COMMAND

This is not really a trick since it has many practical uses, such as warning you when visitors arrive. Watch your pup and try to find out what makes him bark. It may be when he is going for a walk, when you start playing with him, when the doorbell rings, or when he wants his dinner. When your puppy does bark, tell him "Speak" and reward him. Put a lot of enthusiasm into it since you want him to be excited. Even if it takes a while, this is well worth teaching. In fact, the easiest way to stop a noisy dog from barking is to teach him to bark on command— and then teach him to stop barking!

HIDE-AND-SEEK

This is a great game for puppies to play with children. Start off by letting the children hide. Most dogs will enjoy "sniffing" them out. When they can do this, you can progress to hiding a toy or some other object. This will be easiest with the retriever breeds, who love holding something in their mouths. Start by throwing the object out a short distance where the puppy can see it and then send him to fetch it.

RETRIEVING

If you want the retrieving instinct to develop it should be encouraged at the earliest stage. Otherwise, if you ignore or don't encourage the puppy to pick things up and bring them to you, he will probably stop bothering to retrieve at all.

On the other hand, the puppy with the retrieving instinct might bring you something "undesirable"—one of your best shoes, or a very dead, very smelly rabbit when you are out for a walk. Your natural reaction could be to scold the puppy for being "naughty." However, just as puppies have to learn to control their natural reactions, so must we. While the retrieving instinct is developing, the puppy must be praised every time he shows any inclination to pick something up. Once he retrieves on command, he should only be rewarded when he retrieves in response to your order to do so.

There are several methods of teaching the "Retrieve," but the best way concentrates on playing. Children can often encourage a puppy to retrieve far quicker than their parents. They are less inhibited and do not feel they are "making fools of themselves" by getting on all fours to encourage the puppy to play. However, the children must be supervised. A puppy will not learn to retrieve if the children throw a ball and then chase him all around the garden trying to grab it back.

The object you use to teach "Retrieve" does not really matter, as long as you choose something that the puppy likes and which is easy to carry. Never try to force him to pick up something which he obviously dislikes. Use something which is easy for both of you to hold, such as a stuffed sock or a soft toy. Oddly enough, it is much easier to teach a puppy to let go of something he likes than to teach him to hold on to something which he would rather spit out! If the puppy refuses to release the object, a treat offered on a fair exchange basis will usually persuade him to let go.

Reward your dog for every object she retrieves, even if it is a forbidden object (in which case, substitute an allowed toy).

6

GROWING UP

Puppies are disciplined by their mother for as long as they are with her. If this discipline is continued by the new owner, the pups are less likely to cause trouble when they become "teenagers" than those who have been allowed to run wild. In the early stages, most training can be applied by reward, but later on some correction will almost certainly be necessary.

Reaching Adolescence

The age at which a puppy becomes adolescent varies between breeds and individuals of the same breed. Generally speaking, small breeds mature more quickly than large ones. Yorkshire Terriers are quite often as mature at six months as some Irish Wolfhounds are at two years. The level of testosterone, especially in the male, is at its peak at about this time. Quite suddenly, this can make the pup feel "grown up" and that there is much more to life than obeying his owner. The opposite sex becomes more interesting and the marking of territory more important. Signs of dominance may appear for the first time, and sometimes aggression, especially toward other dogs.

The In-Season Female

The beginning of adolescence in the female is when she first comes in season ("in heat"). The age at which this happens varies considerably, from as early as six months to twelve months or older. This can be a traumatic experience for her. Not only does she have to cope with hormonal changes which affect her both mentally and physically, her lifestyle must also change. For a start, she will have to be kept away from male dogs. Suddenly, and for no reason that she can understand, she is in isolation, separated from dogs she may have been with since puppyhood. Not surprisingly, the behavior of some females changes dramatically at this stage, and occasionally the change is permanent. You need to be patient and loving; play games and spend time with her so that she knows that she is still a valued member of the family.

The Case for Neutering

The Humane Society of the United States estimates that 4–5 million cats and dogs are euthanized each year. Unwanted litters are a huge part of this problem. Unless your dogs are intended for breeding, please consider having them spayed or neutered. This is a simple procedure performed by a vet. Most local humane associations and shelters offer financial help for families who otherwise could not afford to spay or neuter their pets. Many people also notice that their pets are better companion animals after being spayed or neutered since hormonal surges are minimized, making the animal less likely to mark territory or be aggressive.

Neutering can be a benefit to the animal too; it removes the frustration of wanting to follow natural breeding instincts but not being allowed to. Spaying also eliminates a number of serious health risks, including tumors of the reproductive organs.

Most vets recommend spaying and neutering at around four to six months of age, prior to the onset of puberty. However, it is possible to perform the procedures as early as eight weeks of age although the long-term benefits and risks of this are still being examined.

Coping with Bad Behavior

Just like teenagers, your adolescent dog will have good days and bad days. You will have to learn to live with this for a while and make the most of the good days. Sometimes your dog will behave like an overgrown puppy, and other days he will think he is a "big macho dog" and not obey you at all. When this happens, do not fight for control—it will only make matters worse. Above all, never give a command that is likely to be ignored and which you cannot enforce. The best remedy is to play with your dog—games such as chasing a ball or playing hide-and-seek with a favorite toy—and make sure he is getting plenty of exercise. If the dog persists in doing things that you cannot allow, put him on a leash, say the command "Down," and make sure he stays in that position for a reasonably long period.

The aim of every dog owner should be to train their dog to be a well-behaved member of society, with the adaptability to handle a wide variety of situations.

Young dogs have a very short attention span. Keep training sessions short and cheerful, always ending on a positive note. You will achieve far more this way than if you keep nagging at your dog in long, tedious training sessions.

Avoiding Temptation

The adolescent dog finds it almost impossible to resist temptation, so the best course of action is to try and avoid situations where your dog is likely to disobey house rules. Do not give her the opportunity to steal the roast off the table by leaving her alone with it. If you are going out without your dog, make sure you do not leave her in a room where she can tear up your best rug. When your cat is sunning himself in the garden, do not let your dog out so she can chase the cat. The last thing you want at this stage is a showdown. Confrontation will start a battle of wills, and all the good work you have done building a relationship with your dog will be ruined. The vast majority of young dogs soon settle down, and peace and harmony are restored to the household.

A puppy needs to learn his place in the family.

Praise and Stimulation

If you spend time socializing and training your puppy through his early days, the rewards will be huge. It is important to bear in mind that we all work better when we are praised, so never forget to reward and praise your dog for doing the right thing, even after he has been trained and has performed the exercise correctly on innumerable occasions. After all, why should your dog try to please you if he gets nothing in return?

Like humans, a dog never stops learning. The more you teach your dog, the more he will learn and the happier he will be. Try to make sure he has something to do—fetching your slippers, fetching the mail, barking to alert you when the door bell rings, etc. When you go out for a walk, vary the route you take and give your dog something different to do, such as searching for a ball, jumping or retrieving. All these things help form a bond of friendship between you, and also ensure that your dog is stimulated and occupied rather than bored and looking for mischief.

A bored dog is certain to get into trouble, whereas a well-trained, well-balanced dog will be a pleasure to you and your family for the duration of his life.

Additional Resources

The American Kennel Club
www.akc.org

American Veterinary
Medical Association
www.avma.org

The American Society for
the Prevention of Cruelty
to Animals (ASPCA)
www.aspca.org

www.aspca.org/aspcakids
Children will enjoy this
site set up by the ASPCA.
It includes games,
cartoons, fun facts, music,
videos, and a section on
dogs under Pet Care.